Father-Son Accountability:
Integrity Through Relationship

John Fort & Lucas Fort

www.johnwfort.com

Copyright © 2015 John W Fort

ISBN: 1508925011
ISBN-13: 978-1508925019

CONTENTS

TO FATHERS

This wasn't an easy book to write. My son and I had to risk being dangerously vulnerable with all of you. My father, though he was a good man and dedicated father, shared none of this information with me. It was not his fault that I ended up becoming addicted to pornography and sex, but it is quite likely he could have saved me from that fate if he would have dared to intervene. He probably didn't know how.

I began working on my own issues related to pornography before my son was born. I eventually became a pornography addiction recovery specialist. Even with that, I did not feel particularly prepared to help my son. He was just a kid, not an addict. Yet, as prolific and pervasive as online pornography had become, I knew he would need help from someone to have even a chance at escaping its claws. As he approached the age I knew he would start to feel the allure of sex, I set apart a weekly time for us to share about those kinds of feelings.

I took what I have learned in my own recovery, modified it to work in a father-son setting, and then we muddled through. This book contains the things we did that worked. And, yes, it has made a huge difference.

1

WHY FATHER-SON ACCOUNTABILITY MATTERS

Most people I meet agree that teaching our sons accountability is needed. However, I meet very few fathers who actually practice accountability with their sons—even a little.

It is no mystery why. First, we don't know how, because our fathers never talked to us about anything as personal as sexuality. Second, we fear our sons will run away in terror if we start talking about anything to do with sex and sexuality. Third, we fear they may find out how messed up we still are.

Most men I talk to agree that our generation would have been better off if our fathers taught us what sexual purity is and how to achieve it. But many of those same men feel they made it through more-or-less okay in spite of having no help from their fathers. This belief causes many fathers to never "get around to" talking with their sons about purity. Men today spend more time with their sons than their fathers spent with them. Most sons today are more obedient than boys of the last two generations. It may seem like we are doing pretty well already, without having to talk to our sons about something so uncomfortable.

The truth is, teen pregnancy rates are down compared to the previous generation. Youth crime and drug use are also lower today than in the previous generation. It can easily appear on the outside that things are pretty much under control in our sons' generation. Unfortunately, while other statistics are looking better, pornography use and sexual behavior among children are off the charts compared to every other generation in our nation's history.

The fact is, pornography is not what it was in our generation. No generation in the history of the human race has ever faced anything like 21st Century online pornography. The effects of pornography use has changed, especially on children.

Father-son accountability is crucial today because the stakes are higher. The consequences of leaving our sons to navigate these waters alone are greater than any other time in human history. Accountability is no longer optional if we want our sons to achieve sexually fulfilled lives as adults.

The Challenge with Pornography has Changed

21st Century Pornography Affects all Boys

When I ask parents about pornography use among children, the typical response is, "I know it's a problem, but I don't think my kids are using it." The reality I see is virtually all boys view pornography, no matter what kind of family they come from.

"Only 3% of boys have never seen internet pornography."
—CyberPsychology & Behavior, 2008

"When I was attending a Christian college, every male and most female students I knew regularly used internet pornography."
—Anonymous man, age 25, 2011

"I found naked photos of my 15-year-old son and of his girlfriend on his phone, which they had been sending back and forth to each other. And he's in a Christian High School."
—Anonymous mother, 2011

In the 21st Century it is no longer a question of *if* a boy will be exposed to pornography, but *when*. I hear from parents all the time about grade school aged kids seeing pornography on a cell phone

2

on a school bus. Boys don't even have to want to see it, pornography will come to them.

Pornography Today is Not the Same as in 20th Century

Pornography is more violent. It is not uncommon for the first pornographic images a boy sees to be videos that simulate men raping women against their will. 88% of video porn shows physical aggression. This teaches children that sex and violence go together.

Pornography is more graphic. In a world super-saturated with sex, it takes extremes to be noticed. The pornography industry is producing more and more graphic, deviant, and shocking material, in order to be noticed. There are no imaginable sex acts that cannot be easily found online.

> "83% of boys and 57% of girls have seen group sex on the Internet."
> —CyberPsychology & Behavior, 2008

> "69% of boys and 55% of girls have seen porn showing same-sex intercourse."
> —CyberPsychology & Behavior, 2008

Pornography is more interactive. Internet pornography goes far beyond images. Videos, sound and even interactive websites allow users to enter the experience like never before. What this does to ones brain is not hard to imagine. As far as the brain is concerned, it is having sex.

> **Lucas:** I do not have a single friend (boys or girls) who has not admitted to looking at pornography. To the dads out there: do not think for a second that your son has not looked at pornography, even if you think they might be "too young." And for boys, don't feel you are "unusually bad" if you have purposefully looked at pornography. I promise all your friends have too, even if they won't admit it. Don't be afraid to admit you're just like any other boy.

3

There is an unlimited supply of Pornography. In the 20th Century and before, even the largest collectors of pornography had only a fraction of a percent of what is available online today. We cannot run out of things to look at any longer. This creates a continual drive and desire to see more. Just knowing all that is out there creates a level of temptation no generation of boys has ever faced before.

Pornography is instantly accessible. There is no more waiting for next month's subscription of Playboy magazine. There is no more waiting for a large image to slowly download to a computer. Thanks to broadband internet, there is instant access to unlimited content, any time one wants it. This teaches the brain it can have any sexual thing it imagines, right now. This is terribly destructive for a boy to experience and then be faced with a very different reality in marriage. Even if you put morality aside, this destroys any possibility of a fulfilling sex life as an adult.

Pornography comes in endlessly novel forms. There is always a new naked person to look at. There is always a new sex act to see. No matter how long a person continues to view and experience pornography, something new and novel is still waiting around the corner. In the past, when pornography was mostly in print form, we had to keep looking back over the same images we had seen a hundred times before. No one needs to keep looking at the same images over and over any more. Of all the differences between earlier pornography and 21st Century porn, this is the most destructive, because of how it affects our brains.

Viewing pornography is almost always accompanied by masturbation. Masturbation releases dopamine in the brain, giving off the highly-pleasing sensation intended to be the reward of sex. Normally, the male body does not continue to crave seeing more of the same nude images after sexual release. After orgasm there is a cessation of desire. This is the way the body was designed to function. This is designed to bond us to our spouse. She is the fulfillment of our desire.

4

However, if there is still an unlimited supply of new and novel nude images to experience, cravings to see more will rebuild. This releases more dopamine into the brain, before the original dose has died off. When dopamine builds up beyond what the body was intended to experience, a binge mechanism is triggered. This causes an almost insatiable and ongoing craving for more pornography.

When our brains are in this binge mode, we are driven to want to keep looking at pornography as long as we possibly can. Our other senses are shut down. Everything else that was important to us suddenly becomes uninteresting. When we are taken away from our pornography, all our brain wants is to get back to viewing pornography. We feel anxious. We feel depressed. We begin to experience little pleasure in anything other than viewing pornography. Even actual sex becomes less interesting than pornography. It becomes more and more difficult for anything to interest us sexually and we look for more deviant forms of pornography.

It is a pretty ugly picture. Repeated exposure to 21st Century pornography turns us into men who want nothing other than to get away from others so we can view pornography. The rest of the time we have a very hard time focusing on anything and feel mostly depressed.

21st Century online pornography "hooks" nearly every male who allows themselves repeated exposure to it. In the late 20th Century, it was estimated that as much as 25% of the adult male population was addicted to pornography. Today, the vast majority of males ages 18-30 use pornography compulsively— constantly craving for more. We have gone from 25% dependence to 90% within a decade.

> "There is a tidal wave of pornography addiction about to overtake our country."
> —Dr Patrick Carnes, leading sex addiction researcher

It Affects Youth Differently than Adults

People under age 25 have brains that are not completely developed. By "not developed" we mean the neural pathways that determine how we make decisions and cope with life have not been "hardened." That is, until our mid-twenties, our brains have only "soft-wired" how they will react to stress and sexual urges. Brains are still very flexible.

Sometime in our mid-twenties, however, we "firm up" whatever neural pathways we have been using **most often** and literally kill off the least used ones. In the case of men who have been viewing high-speed internet porn since they were teens, this means the neural pathways that expect unlimited sexual novelty are cemented. The pathways that would have led to realistic expectations of sex have been cut away. Once that is done, it becomes much more difficult to change how we react to things. Our reactions have become automatic and resistant to change.

Just think of the implications of this. What would that do to a young man who has been binging on pornography since he was 13? I have seen these results first hand when working with young men in their twenties who have developed patterns of compulsive pornography use. They become depressed, have difficulty focusing, and experience heightened levels of anxiety.

I am a support group specialist, not a therapist, but I work closely with a number of therapists who specialize in treating pornography addiction. Sadly, more and more of my peers are seeing children as clients who have been viewing online pornography for years. These children have the same symptoms as children who have been repeatedly sexually abused. This is what exposure to high-speed video porn does to a child. If that isn't enough to frighten us as parents to take action, I don't know what is.

This is not to say that 21st Century pornography does not cause negative symptoms in adults. However, men who were not exposed to this kind of pornography before age 25 are able to pull away from their compulsive use of it much more easily than those who grew up using it. Men who were older when they first saw modern internet porn were never "hard wired" to depend on it. Older men are able to move away from the long list of negative effects faster and more completely.

A Story of Two Generations

Let's look at how this often plays out between generations:

A father who grew up in the 1980s remembers finding pornographic magazines in a friend's older brother's room when he was twelve. The photos were of semi to fully nude women. He saw the images from time to time when he and his friend could sneak a look at them. He was limited to what he could find in a couple of magazines. As an older teen he did come across more pornography, but only a few more magazines. Once or twice he was able to view a pornographic video. While he did continue to have an on and off again desire to look at pornography as a young adult, he moved away from fantasy sex and was more interested in real sex with his wife.

The son of the man above grew up in the 2000s. The son was curious about what sex was so at age 9 he looked up "sex" on the internet when his parents were not home. The internet brought up videos with sound portraying rape-like sex between multiple adults. He was shocked and revolted but also aroused. He vowed never to look at those videos again, but a few days later found himself drawn to view them again, which he did. Soon he was watching online pornography at least weekly. No one else knew what he was watching or how often he was experiencing pornography. He had access to what seemed to him as an unlimited supply of pornographic images and videos. Again and again he drew the line at what he would allow himself to look at, but he always ended up crossing that line and watching more and more obscene pornography. By the time he was 15 he was binging on pornography hours at a time, sometimes all night. By age 25 the son had given up trying to stop looking at pornography and considered it normal. He did not even hide it from his girlfriend. When married, he often had to look at pornography in order to become aroused enough to have sex. His wife was never as exciting as internet pornography and he began to lose interest in actual sex.

Do We Really Want Our Sons to Face this Alone?

When I first sat down to write this book I interviewed a large number of young people, both men and women, in their early twenties. My education is in science, with a masters degree in biology. I knew enough about research to doubt the validity of some of the surveys and statistics thrown around about pornography use in teenagers. However, during these interviews I was appalled by what I heard. The amount of pornography use they described in their teenage and young adult years was astounding. These young people came from caring, supportive families. They could talk to their parents about everything...except pornography and sex.

As I talked with these young people, it was clear that the experience had affected them deeply. The carefree attitudes they had when I first sat down with them often morphed into gloom and despair as they described their teenage years. It was so depressing I had to stop writing for nearly a year. It felt like there was no hope for them. Until, that is, I realized that all of them were desperate to talk about pornography and sex. All of them, every single one, said they wished their parents would have talked to them about pornography.

"75% of children said their parents never talked about internet pornography with them."
— Put Porn in its Place, *Psychologies*, 2010

"My parents and I never had an actual talk about pornography. There was a time I got caught at age 15 which was followed by a talk that was, 'glad you like women, but this is wrong,' and that's about it."
—Anonymous 23 year old male, addicted to pornography, 2013

Talking about pornography and sexual purity with our own children is really hard. It is embarrassing. To do it right, we have to share the struggles and failures we have had. We fear our sons will not respect us anymore, once they learn we are weak too. If we are honest with our sons, we may have to be honest with our wives about things we don't really want them to know. Our marriage could be strained. There are lots of reasons, even valid ones, for avoiding this.

Our fathers, grandfathers and great grandfathers rarely discussed pornography or sex with their sons, other than perhaps to say "don't do it." Which we all ignored. But we know very well the damage that did to our generation. Our generation created online pornography! To continue ignoring what pornography does to teenagers is bad enough. But the stakes are far higher now. 21st Century pornography is hundreds of times more dangerous than what we could find in our childhood. To refuse to help our sons is to sentence them to a life enslaved to pornography, depression and lack of real pleasure.

> "Accountability is an absolute must for those who want to escape the bondage of pornography and never go back."
> —Clay Crosse, *I Surrender All*, 2005

We do not have to be experts to start this. We do not even need to have our own act together first. This is a journey that a father and son can take together. The father will need to be the one taking the initiative, but that is about all he needs to start the process.

> "A boy learns who he is and what he's got from a man...he cannot learn it any other place. He cannot learn it from other boys, and he cannot learn it from the world of women."
> —John Eldredge, *Wild at Heart*

Lucas: I was blessed with an awesome dad who I know loves me and wants what is best for me. Knowing that, I was accepting toward my dad when we first talked about pornography. Before, I had been looking at it online, and not telling anyone. I think God must have put it on both of our hearts, because it wasn't long that he asked me if I was. I immediately said, "No," because I was clearly the best son ever. Yet God kept putting it on my heart to talk to him.

One day, I finally talked to him. I was scared for sure; What if he tore me up? What if he was angry or disappointed? My fears were put to rest when he greeted my mess-ups with open arms. He had the perfect combination of understanding, love, warmth, discipline and teaching. He didn't lecture me—he told me his story. He didn't blow up in my face—he lovingly talked and prayed with me.

"The talk" needs to be had, but with love, understanding, and acceptance. That isn't to say that dads should be uncharacteristically emotional and sappy, making their sons uncomfortable. There still needs to be a sense of authority, saying, "I know what I'm talking about, and I do understand." But, dads should still hold onto some of the sentiment; "It is because I understand that I still and will always love you."

Even though there is a slight potential for fathers to lose the respect of their sons by opening up about their own mistakes, it will at the very least put the thought into their mind of, "Maybe my dad actually knows what it's like."

For the boys: It is vital that you are open with your fathers completely! Doing accountability with your dad will bond you closer to him than you imagine. If or when your dad is vulnerable and opens up to you, that doesn't mean he is weak or "not cool," it simply means he *cares* about you and what you are going through. Your dad wants you to be open too! Accountability is not a one-way street. Be open, be ready, and *help* each other; it takes a team effort!

All in all, I believe trust, honesty, and acceptance is the answer to it all.

2

NEEDS-FOCUSED ACCOUNTABILITY

Up to this point we have only discussed why it is so important to enter accountability with our sons. We have not discussed what accountability actually is. Accountability is one of those loaded words that sometimes causes negative reactions. It is also a word used to describe a broad variety of relational situations. In the case of a fathers and sons, we need a kind of accountability that strengthens the relationship between them. It would be damaging to employ a method that sets a father and son at odds with each other. Not every accountability method works with fathers and sons.

> "If you have sinned, you should **tell each other what you have done.** Then you can pray for one another and be healed."
> —James, the brother of Jesus, *James* 5:16 (CEV)

> "Be kind and compassionate to one another, **forgiving each other,** just as in Christ, God forgave you."
> —Paul, *Ephesians* 4:32 (NIV)

> "Brothers, if someone is caught in a sin, you who are spiritual should **restore him gently.** But watch yourself, or you also may be tempted. Carry each other's burdens, and in this way you will fulfill the law of Christ."
> —Paul, *Galatians* 6:1 (NIV)

We also want to choose a method that works well in sexual purity situations. For that reason, we will use a newer method called *Needs-Focused Accountability*. This may differ from what some have come to think of as accountability.

Needs-Focused Accountability is about:
- coming out of isolation
- building relationship
- moving toward something
- focusing on meeting needs

Needs-Focused Accountability is NOT about:
- punishment
- catching each other doing something "wrong"
- stopping negative behavior

Needs-Focused Accountability is not about pornography and sexual behavior. Not for fathers, and not for boys. The dangers of present-day pornography may be the motivating factor that convinces a father to do accountability with his son, but it is not the central focus once accountability starts. While that may seem counterintuitive, or even "soft," this method has actually shown far better long-term results than focusing on outward behavior. And as for the "soft" part, most men find Needs-Focused Accountability more difficult and frightening than just focusing on behavior.

Steps of Accountability

Both fathers and sons need to record what it is they are agreeing to be accountable for doing. You can write it on paper or put it on your phone, just record it somewhere so you can remember what you are trying to live up to.

Exactly what to write will be covered later. We will call these written records "Accountability Lines." This terminology is used to indicate a "line" we agree to be held accountable to. In a sense, we are saying, "I agree to meet at least this line of behavior." You can, of course, call it something else if you like, but we will refer to these as Accountability Lines in this book.

When it is time to do accountability with your son or father, get out your written accountability line and read directly from it. Don't try to recall what you wrote from memory.

We need to meet together *weekly* for formal accountability. The meeting needs to be face to face. We need to be free from distraction, not while we are trying to watch TV or the like. It is encouraged to check in less formally more often, but a weekly meeting is required to go over all the points on our written accountability line.

We always try to focus on the positive, not failure. Progress cannot be made if we keep our focus on what we are trying to stop doing. No one moves forward by focusing on "not doing" something. Our goal in life cannot be to "not look at porn." Our goal needs to be something we are moving *toward*. What we are moving toward will be discussed shortly.

Step 1—Moving Away from Lust

Pornography is not the problem, lust is. If that is true, we need to understand what lust is and is not. Seeing a naked woman is not lust. In fact, seeing a naked woman, in and of itself, is not necessarily a sin. Before anyone gets angry at that statement, let me tell a story.

> **John:** When I was sixteen there was a job I had to do that required a truck, which my family did not have. My uncle had a truck and gave me the key to his house. I was to let myself in and get the truck key off a hook in his kitchen.
>
> I came in very early one Saturday morning, trying to be quiet and not wake him up. My uncle had recently married and his new wife was young and quite attractive. As I was retrieving the key from the kitchen I heard a gasp behind me. I spun around to see my new aunt a few feet away from me. Completely naked. Even though this woman was new to me, she was technically my aunt. I did

not want to feel excited about seeing her, she was technically my aunt after all, but I could not help myself. Because it was my uncles wife, however, I somehow managed not to carry the image with me and fantasize about it later.

Seeing her naked was not a sin. I had nothing to do with why I saw her and it was not my fault that I did. Getting a little excited at the sight of a naked woman was not my fault either. After all, God designed men to get excited at the sight of a naked woman.

So, where is lust in all this?

If I had captured that image of her and recalled it in my mind later, that is moving in the direction of lust. If I had replayed her image over and over, imagined touching her or imagined having sex with her, then I would have definitely moved into the territory that we call lust. Lust is not an action, it is what we allow to happen inside us.

Perhaps that may seem like an easy out. Perhaps we fear that this kind of definition allows us to "look" and claim to not sin. But when Jesus describes lust, he does not give us any easy outs.

"I say to you that everyone who looks at a woman with lust for her has already committed adultery with her in his heart."
—Jesus, *Matthew* 5:28 (NIV)

If we make accountability to be about what we outwardly do, we are missing the point. If we (fathers and sons) ask each other if we looked at porn during the last week, and leave it at that, we have accomplished nothing. It is not much of an accomplishment to say we did not look at pornography if we *did* spend hours fantasizing about having sex with another woman.

Here is another story that illustrates this point. I was working with a young, married man who was enslaved to pornography. At first, he was reluctant to admit he had much of a problem, though he did not deny looking at pornography. In our discussions he told me

14

that he had never once masturbated before he got married at 23. He had heard somewhere at church that masturbation was bad, so he determined not to do it.

However, he had started looking at internet pornography at age ten. Through middle school and high school he spent hours looking at very hard-core pornography at night. Sometimes stayed up all night. But he managed to never masturbate. That sounds nearly impossible to me, but he assured me it was true. In his mind, the fact that he had not masturbated meant it wasn't that bad. The truth is, which I helped him see, the hours of lust going on in his mind was far worse than masturbation. As far as his brain was concerned, he was having sex with thousands of women.

> "You blind Pharisee! First clean the inside of a cup,
> and then the outside will also be clean."
> —Jesus, *Matthew* 23:26, (CEV)

Needs-Focused Accountability is about cleaning the *inside* of the cup. Sure, we will talk about our behaviors, but our focus will be about what is going on inside us. That is a lot scarier than talking about what others can see on the outside. But it is also the only way to produce real change.

Becoming Known to Each Other

Revealing our insides is the only way for a father to truly know his son. It is the only way for a son to truly know his father. Each one likely is afraid for the other to find out what is going on inside. Each one is afraid he will not be accepted if he lets his insides be seen. But for a son to be accepted after letting his father see his inner thoughts is the ultimate experience of being accepted. For a father to be respected even after revealing his inner thoughts to his son is the ultimate respect.

> "He who conceals his sins does not prosper, but whoever
> confesses and renounces them finds mercy."
> —King Solomon, *Proverbs* 28:13 (NLT)

In this way, both father and son come out of isolation and begin building a true and deep relationship with each other. I can tell you, as frightening as it was to let my son know who I really was inside, it was worth the risk a hundred times over. I have no more secrets from him. There is nothing left that I hope he doesn't find out. It is all out. Rather than respect me less, my son respects me *more*.

> **Lucas:** It's the same for me too. Because I opened up to my dad, and he accepted me and I *knew* that he did, I couldn't wish for a stronger relationship between us.

Knowing what my son struggles with has not made me love him less, it has caused me to love him more. I do not feel he is a failure if he slips, I feel he is a success because he is really working on his sexual purity. I feel honored that he does not hide his thoughts from me.

Lust VS Normal Reaction

Doing accountability with my own son, I find myself again and again helping him understand that some things he feels guilt or even shame about are not lust and not even sin. Because we have learned to be open, he tells me when he thinks he has "messed up." Sometimes, he didn't really mess up, he is just afraid he did.

I remember him telling me he had failed when he saw a bunch of girls in gym class who were wearing "short shorts." I could have passed over his comment and said something lame like, "well, try harder next time son." Instead, I asked questions. Did he stare at them? Did he fantasize about them later? Did he try to flirt with them? He had not done any of those things. He wanted to stare at them, and that bothered him, even though he looked away. He felt his heart speed up and a tinge of sexual excitement and thought that must be lust.

His revelation changed the conversation completely. My son had not sinned or committed lust. His body had simply reacted the way it was supposed to. It is unfortunate that our society forces our children to be faced with so many things that cause them to become aroused, but the reaction is both normal and healthy. Sexual interest in not lust. It is only fair that our sons understand this.

Much of the accountability I do with my own son is discussing together what is sin and what is normal reaction. It has even been helpful to me. It is not helpful for any of us to be feeling shame about who God made us, as men, to be.

To live in a state of worry and shame, fretting about becoming aroused by things we cannot control, is enslavement, not freedom. When we feel shame about how the body God designed for us reacts, we live dominated by sin, even when we are not actually sinning. One of Satan's tricks is to cause us to feel shame for things we have no reason to feel shame about.

Addressing lust is a complex issue that will take years for you and your son to work through. What is lust and what is biology? What do we need to repent of and what should we admit but not feel shame for? Fathers, do not pretend you know all the answers. Sons, do not be afraid to bring up even the smallest incident that causes you to wonder if what you've done was sin or just being a man.

Step 2—Understanding Relational Needs

"The bottom line is, how can we be accountable to anyone or any group if we don't know how to share our feelings?"
—Dr. Mark Laaser, *The 7 Principles of Highly Accountable Men*

Determine Most Important Needs

The second focus in father-son accountability is understanding our feelings and relational needs. Men tend to not be particularly good at understanding our own feelings, much less our needs. That in no way means we cannot understand them, it just means that most of us will be new at this for a while.

There are two ways we can think of needs. One is to think

17

about what we need at an emotional level. Sometimes men find it hard to identify these. The other way is to flip it around and consider which negative emotions hit us the hardest, and say that we need to *not* experience these.

We will list both ways of looking at needs here, side by side.

The Most Basic Human Needs:	Our Primary Needs are:
—Dr. Mark Laaser,	To not feel disliked
The Seven Desires of Every Heart, 2008	To not feel misunderstood
To be heard & understood	To not feel ridiculed
To be affirmed	To not feel ignored
To be blessed	To not feel disregarded
To be safe	To not feel rejected
To be touched	To not feel left out
To be chosen	To not feel excluded
To be included	To not feel disrespected
	To not feel abandoned

In our father-son accountability, we each need to determine which of these are the needs that affect us the most when they are not met. Perhaps these are the ones we notice most often or the negative feeling hits us the hardest. These are not exhaustive lists, just something to get us started thinking.

Let us be clear on this point, these are not *wants,* they are things we really *need.* We were designed to be social creatures. The human race is not a solitary one. While we sometimes compare men to lions, we are nothing like lions. Human males do not leave society after mating and wander alone as male lions do. We are like wolves, tied tightly together in community and with other men. We are designed to be social and things go sideways very quickly when we isolate.

"Two are better than one, because they have a good return for their labor: If either of them falls down, one can help the other up. But pity anyone who falls and has no one to help them up. Also, if two lie down together, they will keep warm. But how can one keep warm alone? Though one may be overpowered, two can defend themselves. A cord of three strands is not quickly broken."
—King Solomon, *Ecclesiastes* 4:9-12, (NIV)

Relational Needs Drive Lust

If our aim is to avoid lust, the most powerful thing we can do is to make sure our relational needs are being met. When our emotional needs are met, we are far less likely to feel sad, lonely or beat up. When our emotional needs are not met, we crave comfort. There are few things that are as immediately comforting as pornography and lust. The chemicals given off in our brains when we are aroused have nearly no equal in their ability to block unpleasant feelings.

"Notice that the struggle with pornography or masturbation is most difficult when you are lonely, or beat up, or longing for comfort in some way."
—John Edlredge, *Wild at Heart*

Males learn very early that fantasy, pornography and masturbation eliminate negative feelings. At least, they do for a very short time. Our brains remember this experience, even if we do not consciously think in this way. As soon as we feel bad, or brains begin to scream at us, "Hey, I know a way to make these bad feelings go away!"

> **John:** I have no memories as a boy of thinking, "Hey, I feel sad, I think I'll go look at pornography and masturbate." However, when I look back at myself in middle and high school, I can see that the times I did were often when I was, in fact, sad and feeling alone. At first, pornography was mostly just new and exciting to look at and masturbation just felt good. But very quickly those things became what I did when I felt rejected.

If we begin to track the times we feel tempted, we will soon notice that temptation comes most often when we feel left out, forgotten, shunned, or that we have failed in some way. For men, and boys, who cannot understand why temptation seems to hit them for no reason, it can be freeing just to discover that there are very predictable times when we feel tempted.

19

Lucas: One thing that I try to do is that whenever I feel sad, angry, lonely, etc., I share those feelings with my dad once they spark up. Even if I don't know what it is that is making me feel that way. By doing this, I can talk about it and usually walk away feeling better and not have to even think about doing anything sexual. Give it a try!

Both fathers and sons may not be sure which of their relational needs requires most help. In that case, simply guess which two or three need the most help and start there. In time we can determine if we need to change our focus to a different need. We just need some place to start.

Some fathers figure out how this works rather quickly. Fathers who have already done some work on understanding what needs drive their feelings are ahead of the game. Then again, some fathers have been suppressing emotions for decades and may find it very difficult to connect to their feelings and needs.

Younger sons, ages 14 and below, can find the connection between needs and lust confusing. Boys those ages can have a hard time determining how they feel at all, much less what need is driving their feelings. Not to mention, early on in puberty, arousal and lust can occur so easily that at first there may be less of a connection.

Lucas: My dad and I started getting into Accountability when I was about 12. At first, when my dad tried to explain the "needs" section of accountability, I didn't really understand it. I didn't understand that being tempted had anything to do with my emotions. It may seem simple, but in experiences of my own and of friend's, boys don't seem to be very in touch with that correlation. I wasn't in touch with it until I was 14; I realized that I would become tempted because I was sad, or lonely, or something like that. When I finally understood this, the amount of temptations I had went down and down.

The level of testosterone in boys increases nearly 500% during puberty. It takes a couple of years to get used to that drastic of a change. During the first couple of years after puberty a boy may be mainly reacting to external stimuli, rather than unmet relational needs, when he experiences lustful thoughts. That doesn't mean he can ignore his relational needs, it just means it may not make a lot of sense yet.

In time, however, every boy can become aware of what negative relational feelings are driving most of his temptation. We do not wait for this to happen before starting accountability. Fathers and sons alike simply need to be aware that it can take time to figure out all the connections.

To start off with, each of us should select two or three emotional needs that he feels is most important to him. We will use these in the next step.

Step 3—Moving Toward Purity

The last step in accountability is to have a few things that we are working toward doing. Needs-Focused Accountability differs from some methods in that it focuses more on what we are moving toward than what we are moving away from. These are things that will take the pressure off trying to avoid lust. There are lots of things we may want to have as goals, but in accountability we want to focus on those things that affect our sexual purity. Because unmet relational needs have the greatest negative impact on sexual purity, those are the most important things we focus on changing.

Look back at the needs you identified as the ones you think you need most work on meeting. Upon writing this booklet, mine were: being valued and being wanted. Notice that "being wanted" is not in the list I shared. I just made it up because it seemed to fit me better than the others. Feel free to work outside the lists given previously. A father and a son may not have the same needs listed on their respective accountability lines, nor should they.

What goals could I put in place to meet those needs? What things could I agree to be held accountable for doing on a regular basis? How often will I agree to do them? Be specific.

Feeling valued can only happen within relationship. Another person is required. The same is true of feeling wanted. Exercise will not help me feel more valued. Eating right will not make me more wanted. We can have those goals, but they do not directly help me with relational needs.

What Does Meet Relational Needs?

Relationships are the only thing that can meet relational needs. In other words, as crazy as it may sound, the number one way to break free from the power of lust is to engage in more and deeper relationships. However, those interactions have to be face-to-face. It is key for everyone to understand that communication through an electronic device DOES NOT COUNT for relationship. We cannot get our real relational needs met through an electronic device. It may feel a little like real relationship, but it simply won't meet our real needs. That doesn't mean there isn't a place for them, but they play a secondary role.

Looking at online pornography does not meet relationship needs, even though the women we are looking at may, technically, be real people. Those women have no interest in us. Reading and writing social media posts does not meet relational needs either, even though there are real people on both ends of the communication. On social media, we present to each other an artificial image of what we want people to see. Social media is not two real people interacting, it is interaction between artificial representations of people. Neither meets any real needs. Sure, it can temporarily feel relational to look at porn or use social media, but we do not come away feeling truly known and loved, which is what we need from relationship.

In order to get our needs met, in order to break free from the power of lust, we need to spend more time interacting face-to-face with people. And, just to be clear, many parents spend more time on their mobile devices at home than their kids do. This is not just a problem with teenagers. Our accountability lines must contain something about interacting with people face-to-face.

Who Meets Relational Needs?

Fathers and sons will already be spending more time with each other as they do accountability. This will meet some of both of your needs, especially for the son.

> "When a father and son spend long hours together, which some fathers and sons still do, we could say that a substance almost like food passes from the older body to the younger."
> —John Eldredge, *Wild at Heart*

However, neither of you can meet all of each other's relational needs. Fathers and sons both need other relationships as well. You will both need other places you can practice being real. Fathers, in particular, need other men that they do accountability with, besides there son. It is not fair to expect a son to be the sole person a father is responsible to.

Second, although it is usually women who men and boys lust after, it is not fair to expect women to meet all of our relational needs. The biggest need men and boys have revolves around being validated as men.

> "Femininity can never *bestow* masculinity."
> —John Edlredge, *Wild at Heart*

It can feel easier to spend time with women, but they can never give us validation as men. Only another man can do that. But being open with other men can be frightening. What if they find out who we really are? What if they think we are posers? What if the don't validate us?

There is no reward without risk. To have our need for validation met, we have no alternative but to risk being invalidated. This is exactly why most men and boys give up and turn to pornography and fantasy. Pornography and fantasy never invalidate us. But they always leave us feeling like frauds, because we are frauds when we use them. We are left with a single alternative, to enter the world of men and allow ourselves to be known.

That does not mean we have to go find some male friends and immediately tell them all our dark secrets. That would be unwise. But we can at least stop lying. We can share a little with them. We can tell them when we feel sad or rejected by someone else.

John: Whenever I see that I am becoming close friends with another man, I always tell them about my past. My past is full of sexual sin. I figure, they're going to find out eventually if they keep hanging out with me, so I might as well find out if he's going to reject me now, rather than waste both our time. So far, every single man who I have told this to has admitted that he has or still does, struggle with lust. Of course, someday I'll meet someone who rejects me for this, but at that point I'll have enough men who validate me for having the courage to be real, that it won't matter if one or two reject me.

My personal accountability line includes a "Move Toward" item I call, "actively seeking connection with other men." When I do accountability with my son, I report on whether I actively attempted to spend time with another man that week, outside of normal activity. Did I ask someone out for lunch or coffee? Did I go to a friend's house? Did I invite a friend to come hiking with me on the weekend? Did I at least call someone and talk?

Lucas: One item on my accountability line says, "more time face-to-face than by text." That means I have to spend more time talking face-to-face with a friend than by text.

One of the biggest reasons that I put that on my accountability line is because whenever I spend more time on my phone than with those friends in person, I end up getting annoyed with them. Because of the false reality tied into social media that my dad talked about earlier, when I text friends consistently more than I talk to them face-to-face, they text me things that I know are not true; I find that out when I do hang out with them face-to-face. I have been "blessed" with an ability to see people's emotions better than most people. So when I hang out with someone at a coffee shop and they are silent the whole time, but then when they text me they practically spam my phone with texts, I feel lied to and cheated on. That's why I also stay away from having my only relationship with a person be over texting—because I know that what they seem like on the phone is not who they really are.

Other Ways to Meet Relational Needs

In addition to relational activity, there are a couple of other things we can do that help with relational needs. Keeping a log of things we are grateful for or positive things that happen helps us to feel wanted, cared for, loved and so on. Most of us realize that God is supposed to love us. We just don't always feel that loved. When we keep a record of things we are aware of that are good in our lives, it is much easier to see that we are loved. Seeing we are loved is much more powerful than reading about it.

These logs or journals should be very short, listing only a couple of things each day in a bulleted list. Just use a few words, do not bother to write out the situation. If we make it easy to do, we might actually do it.

There is definitely room for digital communication in accountability. The primary use for digital communication is to notify each other when we encounter stress or lust. Rather than wait for our appointed accountability time, both fathers and sons should notify the other any time they feel stress, a negative emotion, are tempted or when they fall into lust. We cannot always call, but we can usually shoot a text out.

It may feel unnecessary, or even weak, to be sending out communication every time we sense a negative emotion, but it is very necessary. As we've discussed, negative emotions, or unmet needs, are the precursors to lust. The sooner we admit them the less likely we are to fall into temptation later.

Of course, we should text or call whenever we see something sexually tempting, like a scantily clad woman. But I have found that it is much more common to have to text my son about how I am feeling.

We are looking for patterns: Something happens – leading to a need – leading to discomfort. Pornography teaches us to automatically turn to lust to cover up our discomfort. We may not even notice feeling temptation before we are floundering in lustful thoughts. This is why we should not wait until we feel tempted to reach out to each other, admitting that we are experiencing a need or unpleasant emotion.

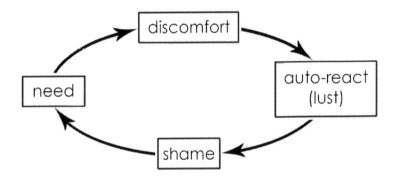

Once we carry out our lust, we feel shame about who we are. Our original need was never met, so we return to it, becoming even more miserable than we started out. If we learn to reach out during the day, when we feel these needs, we can cut off this cycle before it begins.

For example, my son noticed a few years back that the main time he struggled with fantasy was when he was walking home from school. He has an unusually long walk and was usually alone. It is likely that being alone right after school made him feel sad in some way, though he was not able to identify that feeling at the time. All he knew was, he needed help when he walked home from school. So, he began to call me when he was walking home. I was usually able to pick up and talk. I could not talk for the entire time he was walking, but I could for two or three minutes. We did not talk about sexuality or temptation, we just talked about how our days were going. If I could not talk, he just left a message. That was all he needed, his struggle with fantasy went away on his walk home from school.

At the end of each day we can also ask each other how we have been feeling. This does not have to include if we have felt tempted. It is okay to sometimes just talk about feelings. By making discussion of our feelings and needs become an almost daily thing, it takes an enormous burden off of us that would otherwise potentially drive us to escape into fantasy or pornography.

> **Lucas:** Sometimes at school I will start to notice the signs that temptation is coming. Part of the time I am not tempted because I get to class and become indulged in work. Other times, I am tempted anyway. I tend to get extremely tired as the day progresses at school (like any *normal* teenager) so by the time I was home, I forgot about the times I was tempted or getting close to tempted. One thing I try is to write down on paper or my phone when I can tell I might be tempted soon, and have that with me through the day. That way, when my dad asks, "How was your day today?" I can have a better answer than, "Well, I was tired."

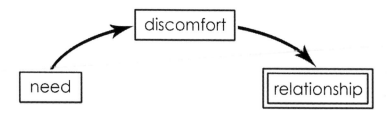

Meeting Other Needs

While unmet relational needs are the main drivers to lust, they are not the only ones. We have a harder time with lust when we are tired, when we are stressed out, even when we have accomplished something great and want to celebrate. In additional to doing things to meet relational needs, we can add one or two things to our accountability line that fall under the category of self-care.

You could include things like:
- getting 8 hours of sleep most nights
- celebrate accomplishments by (fill in your own ideas)
- treat yourself to a fancy coffee (or pizza) every Friday
- make time once a month for a favorite activity
- watch a good movie on Saturday nights

A good friend of mine calls these "righteous pleasures." God never intended our lives to be empty of pleasure. God invented pleasure for us to enjoy. If we never allow ourselves pleasure, lust will rear its head to highjack us into destructive forms of pleasure.

When we take responsibility for rewarding ourselves, it forces us to acknowledge that we are worth taking care of. If we feel valuable, we are far less likely to need to escape into fantasy. When we feel taken care of we do not need a fantasy to take care of us any longer.

Living in a Foreign Land

All of this will likely feel strange to us, perhaps more so for fathers. Boys are not set in their ways yet and can adapt to new ways of living more easily. Men, not so much. Talking about feelings all the time feels weird. At first, for me, it made no sense. I tried to understand how I felt but often had no idea. I could say, "I feel bad," but didn't really know about what.

John: I lived in Brazil for two years in my late twenties. There were some Americans to talk to, but on weekends I travelled to a place with only Brazilians who spoke no English. For a long time, every Sunday would end with my head aching in pain from concentrating so hard all weekend to understand what everyone was saying to me. It took nearly a year to be able to understand most of what was being said to me and to speak back in semi-intelligible Portuguese.

Learning to relate to each other in this way, focused on feelings and needs, can feel like moving to a country where we don't speak the language. It may take a very long time to feel comfortable in this new way of relating. We will grow tired and want to return to places that speak our language. That is normal, we just have to not give up. We will become comfortable eventually.

Ask Questions

"I went to a Christian friend whose walk I respected and whose integrity I can trust and asked him to hold me accountable in my daily life. I gave him a free hand to ask me anything about my life at any time. I told him that nothing was off-limits…I asked my friend to always end our talks with the question, 'Have you lied to me in any of your answers?'"
—Clay Crosse, *I Surrender All*, 2005

To make accountability effective, both parties need to be free to question the other. When my son says, "I had trouble the other day," I need to ask questions to find out what he is talking about. If one of us says, "I felt tempted last night," that requires a question or two to find out what we are really talking about.

While we sometimes need to ask questions to bring sin into the light, most questioning should not be about behaviors we are trying to stop. Remember, the focus of accountability is not stopping something. The most important questions we ask are to help each other determine what unmet need drove us to seek the comfort of lust.

We can ask questions like:
- What were you feeling right before that happened?
- What happened around you right before you felt tempted?
- Has there been something you've been avoiding, or that has been stressing you out lately?
- What things have been nagging at you lately?
- What need is created when you feel or experience these things?

Once the need is discovered that started the problem, we can then ask questions to help each other learn alternative ways of dealing with needs. These are the second most important questions we ask.

We can ask questions such as:
- What other thing could you have done to meet that need?
- Is there a time coming up soon when you might feel this need again?
- What is your plan to deal with that need?
- What can I do to help you? How can I be there for you?

Fathers need to step down a little from the parent role and move a little closer to a brother-in-Christ role when questioning our sons. Otherwise, our questioning will feel like an interrogation and shut our sons down. As long as we believe our sons are trying, there is no need to pull rank during accountability.

Sons need to step up into the role of a man and question their fathers. You will not live at home forever (hopefully) and will need to find your own accountability partner. You need to learn how to ask questions now, so you can do it later with your own peers. Besides, your father needs it.

This will feel stiff and unnatural at first, but keep it up until you are both used to this new way of relating. The main point is to have someone you can share any of your feelings with. Even if nothing else is accomplished, asking each other questions proves you are both listening. By doing that, you are both meeting each other's need to be heard and understood.

3

IMPORTANT CONSIDERATIONS

Willpower and Accountability

There are a lot of tricks to be learned from research on willpower and self-control that help significantly in the struggle against lust. We do not have time to go over all of them now, but we can mention one at this point that is important to understand before actually writing an accountability line.

Willpower is the energy we use to make decisions. Any decision we make uses up willpower; deciding to do something we really want to do, as well as deciding to do something we dread. Making a decision we do not really want to make uses up more willpower, as you might imagine, but all decisions drain our reserve.

Each day we start out with a given amount of willpower. We drain that supply all day long with each decision we make. If we are trying to "not do" a long list of things as well as "do" another long list of things, we will very soon run out of willpower. The more things we are trying to do and not do, the faster we will run out of the energy it takes to make those decisions. When our willpower is low or gone, we give in to whatever is the easiest to do. Lust is always the easiest thing to do.

"Decision making depletes your willpower, and once your willpower is depleted, you're less able to make decisions."
—Roy Baumeister & John Tierney, *Willpower*

In order to experience success in an area as difficult as lust, we need to limit our focus to just a few things. It makes sense to focus on the most destructive things first, to get them under control, before worrying about the rest. Even the business community understands that having too many goals is unhelpful.

"You can't have more than three goals, and it's fine if you have less than three. Each week we go over what we did last week and whether we met those goals or not."
—Aaron Patzer, *Mint.com*

For this reason, when you write your accountability line, you will need to limit the list of "Move Away From" items and "Move Toward" items to just two or three items each. Our accountability between fathers and sons will not go beyond that.

For some of us who are perfectionists, this will feel like cheating. Some of us will feel a desire to write a long list of things to move away from and a long list of things to move toward doing. But, research has proven conclusively that long lists do not work and, in fact, cause us to fail faster.

Once we have mastered a particular item, we can cross it off and add something else we need to stop or start doing. That doesn't mean we stop trying to do or not do the things we cross off, we simply do not need to focus on them as much since they have become automatic. Things we do automatically do not use up much willpower at all.

We do need to be careful not to cross something off our list too soon. Let us say that one of our "Move Away From" items is "Do not look at pornography." If we manage not to look at pornography for one month, this is not nearly enough time to be sure we have mastered pornography. We need to have at least six months of doing or not doing an item on our list, with no failures, before considering crossing it off. And, once we do cross something off, if we fail again we probably need to add it back to our list and remove something else to make room for it.

Masturbation

It is difficult to discuss accountability without mentioning masturbation. In Christian circles masturbation is a highly controversial topic. Christians disagree on whether masturbation is sinful always or sinful sometimes. One thing is sure, however—it causes Christians a lot of grief.

> "Regardless of what we call it, masturbation is something the vast majority of men and women deal with on some level. In fact, many find themselves trapped in a cycle of defeat and shame. They try to stop, but they can't. They promise God they'll never do it again, but they fail. Masturbation becomes the defining issue in their relationship with God. They're desperate for answers—are they doing something wrong, or should they just give up trying to resist?"
> —Joshua Harris, *Sex is Not the Problem (Lust is)*

There are highly reputable Christian therapists and theologians who come down on both sides of the fence as to whether masturbation is a sin and harmful or not. In order to look objectively at it, let us consider seven facts about masturbation.

Fact 1: The Bible is silent on the topic of masturbation. While it is quite clear on lust and what goes on in our minds, it says nothing about the physical act of masturbation. The Bible is not silent about other sexually related issues, being fairly graphic and clear, so it is unlikely this silence is due to the embarrassing nature of the topic.

Fact 2: It is not uncommon for very young boys to accidentally discover masturbation without outside influence. These boys have no concept of sex and are not thinking of or looking at anything sexual when they occasionally masturbate. It is typically when they enter puberty that they begin to combine lust and masturbation.

Fact 3: Nearly 100% of teenage boys masturbate on a regular basis. This is not how many boys have *ever* masturbated, but how many do so on a regular basis. This percentage is not lower for boys in Christian homes. There are men who have never masturbated in their life, even as teenagers, but they are very rare.

> "96% of teenage boys masturbate regularly."
> —Dr. Archibald Hart, *The Sexual Man*

Fact 4: Well over half of men continue to masturbate even after they have married. These results come from Christian homes as well, so no one can hide behind religion and pretend church going men are any different.

> "61% [or three out of five] of the married men he surveyed admitted to continuing masturbation after marriage…82% [the vast majority of these men] masturbated about five times per month."
> —Dr. Archibald Hart, *The Sexual Man*

Fact 5: Anything that causes us to feel shame tends to drive us away from God. Shame also causes us to isolate from others and ultimately end up wanting to comfort ourselves again somehow, often in inappropriate ways.

Fact 6: In men and teenage boys, masturbation is usually accompanied by viewing pornography, imagining themselves having sex, or imagining looking at someone naked. The Bible defines these things as "lust" and identifies them as harmful and sinful.

Fact 7: There are some men and boys who masturbate, but do not fantasize or look at pornography at all when they masturbate.

This last fact may seem impossible to many of us. It is true, however. Dr. Doug Weiss describes these men in this way.

"In [this type] of masturbation, the man's decision for his behavior has been made usually between ages twelve and sixteen. When this teenager begins to masturbate, he stays fully 'connected' to himself during the act, i.e., he does not lust or create sexual fantasies…and he would never use pornography when he masturbates. For this boy, the masturbation experience is simply engaging in a bodily function."
—Dr. Doug Weiss, *Sex, Men & God.*

Again, not everyone agrees with Dr. Weiss. Many feel that masturbation, even if it can be done without fantasy, is harmful. Joshua Harris explains it this way:

"Masturbation is built on a self-centered view of sex. This wrong attitude says that sex is solely about you and your pleasure. Your body. Your genitals. Your orgasm. This is the natural tendency of sin. It isolates us from others and makes pleasure self-focused."
—Joshua Harris, *Sex is Not the Problem (Lust is)*

A compelling argument, for sure. Yet, the fact remains that almost all teenage boys will continue to masturbate. What do we do with that? What about the boy who discovered masturbation at age 7 and at age 13 is suddenly having trouble with lust during what used to be a non-sexual behavior?

John: The first time I masturbated had nothing to do with sex at all. I was 13, had just entered puberty, and realized I was old enough to ejaculate and wanted to see what that was like. I was not embarrassed by what I did. I was perfectly aware that God saw me. It did not feel wrong and did not cause me shame to find out how my body worked.

However, very soon after I was adding sexual fantasy to masturbation and within a couple of months pornography became part of the picture. I *did* feel shame about that, and from then on masturbation always left me feeling dirty and bad.

35

Would it have been possible for me to not have added fantasy to masturbation? I will likely never know. The only influences I had back then were boys my age and older who were all using as much pornography as they could find and masturbating frequently to it. They taught me that masturbation was intended for use with pornography, so that's how I used it.

For me today, as a married man, masturbation is simply not something that can be part of my life any longer. I did struggle with it early in my marriage, but after counseling and accountability with other men, I have left that behind. I have heard married men say they think it's okay to masturbate when their wife is temporarily unavailable, but to me that smacks of selfishness. Perhaps it is more understandable for a man when a wife is unavailable for a very long period of time, but I'm not sure I want to be the one to condone that.

The problem is, we are all affected by lust in slightly different ways. What causes one man, or teenager, to lust is not always the same as what causes another to lust. For me, personally, where I am today, masturbation is not okay. Masturbation just has too much lust associated with me. I have too long a history of combining masturbation with lust. I'm not sure I could go back and reclaim that activity and separate it from lust and it is too dangerous to try. Fathers need to be honest with themselves in this area. If masturbation comes with lust, it must be removed.

It is more complex when we talk about teenagers. Try to remember being twelve or fourteen or sixteen. Can you remember how overwhelmingly strong the urge to masturbate was? Is it better for a boy to try not to masturbate, only to break down and end up fantasizing and masturbating anyway? Or, worse yet, end up like the young man I mentioned earlier who never masturbated at all but spend hours looking at hard-core porn and lusting since he was 10.

"It is a mistake to make the act of masturbation the measure of our relationship with God. If you believe that masturbation is wrong, do you minimize other sins as a result? When you detect arrogance or

> see self-righteousness in your life, do you respond the
> same way as when you [masturbate]?"
> —Joshua Harris, *Sex is Not the Problem (Lust is)*

Joshua Harris believes that masturbation is bad for everyone and always falls into the category of sin. Even with this viewpoint, he points out that we cannot put masturbation into a "more serious" category of sin than something like being prideful. If we do, Satan will use that against us, causing us so much shame that we give up trying to move forward. We end up falling away from God over an activity that the Bible does not even name as a sin.

We cannot get around the fact that 96% of our sons are going to masturbate sometimes, no matter how hard they try not to. This is no different from recognizing that 100% of all of us are going to sin again, probably in the near future. But, God is faithful to forgive us of our sins, this we also know. We need to treat the act with the appropriate level of concern. The act of masturbation is far less of a concern than entertaining lustful thoughts.

Lucas: The first time I masturbated was because I realized that I was old enough to ejaculate, and wanted to find out what it was like. Honestly, I was disgusted and vowed never to do it again. That sure worked out like a charm. I ended up doing it fairly often after that.

For a year or two, I never told my dad about the masturbation part of my sexual impurity, only the pornography/lust part. One time, I think because my dad thought that maybe I wasn't telling all of it, he told me about the link between masturbation and lust. After that, guilt kept bubbling up inside of me, and not too much time later, I opened up and told him about how I had been masturbating. It was uncomfortable and not easy, but my dad listened, and told me the facts of it like what is written above.

With some of his help, I began setting rules for myself. I first decided that I felt too ashamed to masturbate, so I chose to try not to ever do it. I soon realized that for my particular case, that was not going to work. I messed up too often. Then, after discussing further with my dad, I set a planned date, one time during the week, where I would masturbate but *not* fantasize at all.

This worked for me for quite a while. Sure, I messed up a few times and gave into temptation, but I talked to my dad and he moved me through it. After not too long a time, I began to find that I didn't even need to masturbate once a week, so I changed it to once every other week. Once a month. Every other month.

I have observed in my work that only a few young, unmarried men are able to completely cease masturbation altogether. More are successful in using masturbation rarely, without fantasizing or using pornography, and do so without the side effect of shame. Others strive to abstain completely, but give in two or three times a year to the temptation to masturbate to pornography or fantasy. These differences do not appear to be a measure of how serious these young men are with their accountability.

No studies have been done about teenage boys in accountability with their fathers, but I suspect we would find similar results. I am not going to tell you what you are supposed to believe about masturbation. Each father and son will have to determine what they are moving away from and moving toward. There are only two things I feel we can conclude for certain:

1. We should move away from masturbation combined with pornography or any kind of fantasy.
2. If masturbation causes shame, it is destructive and something needs to change.

Does that mean we talk about masturbation during father-son accountability? Yes, it does. If we don't keep secrets about masturbation, we don't have to live in shame. No secrets means no shame. We all admit our weaknesses.

I know I would have been mortified to talk about masturbation with my father, or any other adult, when I was a teenager. Not because I didn't have lots of questions about it, but because I was afraid of what they would say if I admitted what I struggled with. However, today's teens and young adults are much more open about talking about personal things. Today's fathers are more likely to be afraid to talk about masturbation than today's teenagers. This is okay to discuss. This is necessary to discuss. My son and I didn't like discussing it at first, but we got over it. You will too.

Managing Arousing Material

As discussed earlier, each of us has a limited supply of willpower to make good decisions with each day. While it may be true that we can resist temptation to look at arousing materials, there is no reason to waste our limited willpower in doing so. The intelligent thing to do is use any help we can get to avoid needing to use up willpower in this area.

Internet filtering and accountability software is simply a must for every man who wishes to maintain integrity. We will not take the time to discuss all the options here, as they change almost monthly. Ask friends what they use or look up one of the major providers of internet safety software. If you feel hesitant to pay for protection, consider if you would be willing to pay for a helmet if your son joined a football team. Do not fall into the trap of wanting the least expensive option. The best solutions are not the least expensive. This is too important of an area to skimp on. Buy a cheaper brand of bread or something if you need to save money.

The internet is not the only place we need protection. Television and movies are full of provocative scenes. We fool ourselves if we claim it isn't really porn so it doesn't matter. Any honest man will admit we don't need outright pornography to push us into lust. Why expose ourselves, and our sons, to images that will leave us struggling when we go to bed? And if you think it's too racy for your son, why would you, his father, watch it? Set an example and do not watch anything you don't want him to watch.

Books can be as bad or worse than pornography. Some men (and boys) find erotic literature more arousing than images. Lust is in the mind so anything that gets us thinking about sexual situations should be avoided. This includes magazines, graphic novels, and any other kind of print or online media.

Fathers do have the decision-making skills to avoid these things on their own, with accountability to keep our focus straight. Teenage boys do not. Fathers have a responsibility not only to discuss these issues with our sons, but to help them avoid these traps.

Decision Making in Teenagers

There has been a lot of research in the past decade on how decision-making works in adolescents. What has been discovered is that young people under 25 do not make decisions the same way older adults do. This is very important to understand when doing father-son accountability.

When we are faced with a decision, our brain sets up something similar to a trial with a judge. One part of our brain, representing desires and wants, argues to give in to desire. Another part of our brain represents cold logic and argues for considering consequences and safety. A third part of our brain acts like a judge, listening to both sides and determining the winner. At that point we make our decision. It is this "arguing" process, by the way, that uses up our willpower.

Mature adults are good at considering the long-term consequences of any decision we make. It's not that we cannot make decisions that will harm us, but we are far better at avoiding those than teenagers. Teenagers are capable of foreseeing consequences, but the "judge" portion of their brains listen far more to their desires than to their logic. Their brains are actually wired, on purpose, to do this.

There are scientific reasons why this is helpful for people under age 25, which are not important here. What is important is that we all, fathers and sons alike, understand that until they reach age 25, our sons will often make choices that follow their immediate desires rather than consider long-term consequences. This is true even if fathers have lectured them for hours about considering consequences.

And all of this is on top of the fact that they have a flood of hormones driving them toward sexual activity that they are still not entirely used to dealing with. The combination of a brain designed to give more weight to desire and new hormones that create arousal when faced with anything even remotely sexual is a lot to fight against.

> **A True Story:** Consider a 14-year-old boy who has been doing accountability with his father for two years. He knows all the reasons why he should avoid pornography. He actually agrees that looking at pornography will harm him and his relationships with others and God. The boy's uncle is visiting for the holidays and staying in their home. One day the teenager is left alone at home and he notices his uncle left his laptop on and open. In an instant, the boy's brain realizes that right in front of him is an unlimited world of pornography, waiting to be explored. The rational part of this brain protests but is completely drowned out by his desire to see a naked woman. He forgets every reason not to look at pornography and indulges. Afterward the boy feels great shame and becomes anxious about the inevitable time when he has to tell his father what he has done.

As we have said, there is no way to ensure our children will not see pornography. It is nearly inevitable that they will. That does not mean that we shouldn't do everything in our power to try to prevent it. But we also must have empathy for times they fail, either with pornography or sexual fantasy.

Let us fathers be honest for a moment. If we were faced with an unprotected computer with access to unlimited pornography when we were 14, would any of us have walked away? Every time? Even when we just had an argument with our parents? It is unfair for us to expect more from our sons than we were capable of doing ourselves at their age. To be honest, most fathers still have trouble with pornography and have no room to judge. It is more effective to act as fellow travelers with our sons in the journey toward purity than to be their judge.

Understand that it is not a boy's fault that he does what appears to be "stupid things" from time to time. Focus on reducing those occurrences rather than just punishing them. That does not mean there cannot be consequences. We can restrict access and keep our children away from unsafe people, but it must be done with at least some collaboration from our sons. And, if we as fathers mess up we may need to restrict our own access or stay away from certain people or places. We are in no way immune from anything we subject our sons to. If a boy feels unloved or not understood after confessing sexual sin, he will never tell his father again when he messes up.

> **John:** As Lucas approached middle school age there was a period of about a year when my wife and I prevented him from spending time at a couple of his friends' homes. My wife had overheard these friends saying things that indicated they had been exposed to sexual content, probably pornography. It wasn't that we didn't trust Lucas, but we knew he was probably too young to walk away if one of them started showing him pornography when he was visiting their home.
>
> This lasted about a year before his friends grew up a little and we felt Lucas was able to walk away if he needed to. None of this was Lucas' fault, but he still felt not being allowed to visit his friends' homes for so long was a "consequence."

There will be times when we have to give consequences, but they should be to protect more than to punish. If we punish our sons for giving in to temptation and looking at pornography, they will stop being open with us and we will not be able to help them move toward purity.

Father-son accountability is inviting our sons into manhood with us. We expect more of them but they can expect more from us. Accountability is allowing them to come up to our level.

A Quick Boost to Self-Control

Research on self-control has revealed a way to strengthen resolve when we feel ourselves wavering. First, we need to have well thought out standards that we want to live up to. We need a vision of becoming men of purity. We must value freedom from lustful thoughts.

Once we have these standards in mind, when we feel weak and tempted to give in to lust, we only have to remind ourselves of who we want to be. This, somehow, lets off much of the pressure to give in to temptation.

A number of research experiments have revealed that people are far less likely to do something they know is wrong if they can see themselves before they do it. In other words, humans seem to experience less temptation when we can see ourselves when we are tempted.

> "Self-awareness always seemed to involve comparing the self to these ideas of what one might, or should, or could be…Self-awareness involves a process of comparing yourself to [your own] standards."
> — Roy Baumeister & John Tierney, *Willpower*

The easiest way to remind ourselves of who were are is simply to look into a mirror.

> "[When] people could see themselves in a mirror, they were more likely to follow their own inner values…"
> Roy Baumeister & John Tierney, *Willpower*

So, look in a mirror next time you feel tempted to give in. It does not mean looking in the mirror always stops us from doing what we believe is wrong, but it greatly increases our chances of doing what we believe is right.

John Fort & Lucas Fort

4

WRITING YOUR ACCOUNTABILITY LINE

Let's take everything we've been discussing and put it together in a simple format fathers and sons can use. You will want to record your accountability line on something you can access easily, since ideally you will refer to it more than once during the week.

Each father and son is going to record his own accountability line. On that record there will be three sections; a "Move Away From" list, a "Needs" list, and a "Move Toward" list.

Move Away From

Label part one of your accountability line "Move Away From." Each of you decide what the most destructive sexual practices or temptations are that you face. It is likely these will be different from father to son.

By destructive, we mean, what sexual things that you sometimes do would harm your relationships the most if they were discovered. Beyond that, which things cause you to feel the most shame after they happen. These are destructive because they interfere with our relationship with God and others.

From this list, each person records only the top two or three most destructive practices you want to move away from. Do not record any more than three. You will not report to each other about any destructive behaviors other than these.

Needs

Label the second section of your accountability line "Needs." Each of you write what you think your most powerful needs are. These will be the needs that, when not met, cause you to be more vulnerable to temptation. This may be the most difficult list to come up with, as we have alluded to before. Remember that we do not have to be completely sure what our primary needs are, we only need a place to start.

I will repeat the same lists of needs here to consider. You may, of course, come up with your own.

The Most Basic Human Needs:
—Dr. Mark Laaser,
The Seven Desires of Every Heart, 2008
To be heard & understood
To be affirmed
To be blessed
To be safe
To be touched
To be chosen
To be included

Our Primary Needs are:
To not feel disliked
To not feel misunderstood
To not feel ridiculed
To not feel ignored
To not feel disregarded
To not feel rejected
To not feel left out
To not feel excluded
To not feel disrespected
To not feel abandoned

Move Toward

Label the third and final section of your accountability line "Move Toward." Here you will list two or three things you can do that help you meet the needs you listed. Only write things that directly address the needs you listed. We are trying to take responsibility for getting our needs met rather than expecting others to do it for us.

Your list must contain at least one behavior that addresses meeting relational needs with men.

Your completed Accountability Line should look something like this:

Accountability Line

Move Away From:
- look at porn
- masturbate to fantasy

My Needs:
- to be valued
- to be heard

Move Toward:
- seek fact-to-face connection with guys
- call or text Dad/son when feel sad or stressed

John Fort & Lucas Fort

5

FATHER-SON CONVERSATIONS

In the ideal world the father begins engaging with the son quite early with things that will be helpful later, when purity is addressed more formally. However, some of us have to start where we are, even if our sons are older. The things that could be done earlier can still be done later as well.

This is not a book about teaching boys about healthy sexuality. There are plenty of books on that already, so we won't discuss those topics. This is a book about using the relationship between father and son to help both achieve a higher level of purity.

Every boy is different, of course, so the ages may or may not fit any individual son exactly. Use it as a general guide rather than a hard and fast timeline.

Ages 5 - 10

The number one thing for a father to do during these younger years is to model for his son how to express feelings and needs. When a father is feeling sad (or any other feeling) he should verbally express that. The father may or may not need to share feelings directly to his son every time, but he should make sure whoever he tells, his son can hear the conversation.

A son needs to hear that his father has feelings and is not afraid to tell someone about them. A conversation could go something like this:

> **Father**: I am feeling kind of sad today.
>
> **Mother**: Why?
>
> **Father**: Well, I'm not really sure. Maybe because I didn't do a very good job on a project at work and I think my boss is unhappy with me.

This assumes that the mother is willing to take part in such a conversation, but hopefully we as fathers can get our wives to participate in conversations like this, so that our children can learn from them.

Note that the father goes on to try to determine *why* he is sad. That is pretty important. We need to learn that sadness, or any other positive or negative emotion, has a source. We may not be able to control the source, but it is good to know what it is. This will help our sons learn to search for reasons for their feelings as well.

A son needs to know he is not responsible for his father's feelings. It's fine to come home and say we are, say, angry about something that happened at work. It is quite another to take that anger out on our family, who had nothing to do with it. If we are angry, it is very natural for young children to believe they are somehow the cause of our anger. We can help by saying things like:

> **Father**: I'm sorry, but I am feeling angry because someone at work did not do their job and now I have to do it for them.
>
> **Son**: I'm sorry, Daddy.
>
> **Father**: No, son, you did nothing wrong. I am not angry with you at all. I'm just telling you how I'm feeling right now. You don't have to do anything to fix it. I will be okay.

A son needs to know he cannot, and should not, try to help his father feel better. You are certainly familiar with the scenario of an angry father coming home and the entire family having to tip-toe around him to keep him from blowing up. Or the father who comes home depressed and mopes around until someone tries to "cheer him up." Our sons are in no way responsible for making us feel better, nor should they be.

When we tell our family, or sons directly, how we feel, we need to also assure them that it is not their job to "fix" how we feel. By telling them this, we remind ourselves to not expect it.

> **Father:** I found out my best friend is really sick. He might not get better. I am really sad about that.

> **Son:** I'm sorry, Daddy.

> **Father:** You don't have to fix it, I will be okay. I just wanted to tell someone that I am sad.

Now, I realize that someone may be reading this and realizing that they have, in fact, been expecting their family to "fix" how they feel. That does not mean all is lost, it just means there is something new to work on.

There are times when we do need something from our family members. My father never hugged me as a kid. I grew up thinking boys weren't supposed to want hugs. The fact is, everyone needs hugs. I had to learn that it was okay to need a hug now and then, and then learn how to ask for one. Let me tell you, that has been a very difficult journey for me. Father's can ask their sons for a hug, and should. By doing so, we teach them that it is okay to have needs and to seek to get them filled ourselves.

> **Father (to his son):** Could I get a hug? I really need one today.

Our goal in this stage is simply to demonstrate for our sons how to share feelings and needs. We know we are making progress when we see them doing what we have modeled for them.

> **John:** I remember when Lucas was in fourth and fifth grade and he would come home from school saying, "I just feel sad today." I know this sounds odd, but I was very happy to hear him say that. Not that he was sad, but that he was not afraid to tell me. I would sit next to him, put my arm around him, and ask him about it. I would not try to fix it, but just assure him that I was still here for him.

Mothers are usually pretty good about stuff like that, but not dads. It is as if dads are afraid they are not manly when they do this with their sons. I am not a wimpy man, ask anyone who has had a confrontation with me. However, I refuse to allow society to tell me it is not manly to be in touch with my feelings. I have found great strength in that, particularly in the area of purity. When I understand how I feel and know why, I know what to do with those feelings. I can meet my needs in a better way than running off to lust to cover up those feelings.

Other than feelings, another thing that some fathers will be confronted with is early masturbation. It is simply a fact that some very young boys discover a new way to make themselves feel good. It is not abnormal for some boys to accidentally discover masturbation as early as pre-school or some time during their elementary school ages. This was not my personal experience, nor my sons, but I hear from parents all the time who are concerned when they discover their boys have begun to do this. Often, the boy does not even try to hide it, because they do not see any shame in it.

The main thing parents need to remember is, a boy this young has no concept of sexuality and is in no way expressing sexuality when he masturbates. He does not have "dirty" thoughts and is in no way perverted. A parent, preferably the father, does need to teach a boy not to do such things in public. It could be pointed out that we do not urinate in public and this behavior falls into the same "private" category. We do not want to teach our children that their bodies are shameful.

Fathers should not try to explain to a boy this age that what he is doing is similar to sex, or connect it with sex in any way. We do not want to make that connection for them so young, or they may begin to connect masturbation to lust before they are mentally able to deal with such information.

A father should have concern if a boy begins to masturbate frequently or in a way that appears compulsive. Children who have been sexualized somehow, through abuse or early exposure to pornography, are also in a different category. In these cases, a well trained counselor who works with children should be sought out.

Ages 11 - 13

As I said, we will not discuss how to have a "birds and the bees" discussion with your son, but it is wise to say a couple of things that may not come up in such a talk. About a year before a son enters puberty it is good for his father to give him permission to have the feelings that he will inevitably have. No one can stop the sexual interest that will overtake a son when testosterone is unleashed within them. We can help by removing any shame that may otherwise come with that.

> **John:** Lucas was already used to the fact that our family had tight restrictions on internet use and what we watched on TV or movies. But when he turned eleven, we had a different kind of conversation about pornography. I told him when he was a little older, perhaps very soon, he would start wanting to see naked people. He looked mortified at the very suggestion. I assured him that all boys become interested in that when they reach puberty, if not a little before. I told him our hormones make us want to see that kind of thing, and wanting to see was not wrong. God made us that way so we would want to get married.

It's a hard conversation to have when a son doesn't really want to think about such things yet. Of course, some fathers discover their sons already want to, and may have, looked at naked images. Still, we need to set the foundation that we are, as men, designed to want to see nudity. We are designed to want to be sexual. Otherwise, children would never be conceived.

But this wanting, in and of itself, is not bad. Wanting a nice car is not bad, but stealing one is. Wanting a nice car, getting a good job, saving up for a few years, and then buying one is a good thing. Lust, outside of marriage, is sort of like stealing sex—we're taking something before we have earned it, so to speak.

> **Lucas:** I remember the day when my dad told me that I would eventually want to start seeing naked women. I wouldn't quite say that "mortified" is the right way to describe how I felt…My inside reaction was more like if I had been standing on the beach and a great white shark jumped out, grew legs, and started chasing me like a blood-thirsty maniac. The utter though of such a horrific thing petrified me to the point of no other. I thought to myself, "How on earth could you suggest I would ever do such a horrific thing?"
>
> It was only a year later that I had been watching a movie, and there was a topless woman in it, and I realized that I did want to see more. I started to fantasize about girls shortly after. At first, I enjoyed the sensation. Then I began to feel ashamed that I was doing that. However, I remembered what my dad had told me, that it is natural for boys to want to do that. I knew that there would be no harm whatsoever in telling him. Yet, telling him was the last thing I wanted to do, because of the anxiety of the matter. It took a bit more time to get to the point of telling him.

The power in this conversation is, it tells the son he is normal. He *will* want to see pornography, that is not even a question. And, we need to be honest as fathers that we have wanted to, and probably did, look at pornography as well.

John: I told my son about the first time I saw pornography. I was only 9, at a friend's house who had found his dad's stash. I told Lucas that when I got a little older, like 12 and 13, I started feeling inside like I wanted to see more pictures of naked women. I knew it was wrong, but I still wanted to. I admitted that I found some pornography when I was 13 and kept it hidden in my room until I left home at 18. My parents never talked to me about pornography, so I ended up looking at it a lot. I felt very shameful and depressed as a result, especially when I went to church, which reminded me I was not living like I wished I would.

Some fathers may fear that sharing these kinds of things might corrupt their son. They may fear that if their son has not yet seen pornography, such a discussion might put bad ideas in their head. I promise, and you already know if you are honest, the idea is going to end up in his head one way or another. Hormones will see to that. As fathers we need to validate our sons by helping them understand these feelings are normal, hopefully before they have them. Then, when they do have them, they will not need to feel so much shame and can come to us to talk about it.

Lucas: As I have said before, the fact that my dad told me that it is natural to want to look at pornography, and that the desire itself is not bad, had *nothing* to do with me eventually looking at it or masturbating. In fact, the truth of it is quite the opposite; since my dad had talked to me beforehand and even during the time I was looking at pornography, fantasizing, masturbating, etc., I knew that if I told him about it and if I was honest, he would be accepting of that and would help me. And that's exactly what happened.

Once a boy admits to his father that he is beginning to have interest in sexuality, it is time to start doing accountability as described in this book. Perhaps it is not every week but once a month if the son does not yet have strong or frequent urges. But, as soon as they do come, fathers should set up a regular meeting time.

During the appointed accountability time set aside, father and son meet somewhere they can talk privately. They take turns reading what is on their accountability line and reporting how successful they were accomplishing the things in their "Move Away From" and "Move Toward" lists. Even if one person fails on a point in the "Move Away From" list, more emphasis is put on how well each met the "Move Toward" list.

Each person also reminds the other what their listed needs are. They discuss how they felt that week in regard to those needs. This is not a "I did well" or "I did poorly" part of the conversations. During the needs discussion, all we talk about was how we felt. Having a negative emotion is not bad, it is part of life. We must begin to move away from always running away from our negative feelings by learning to express when we have them. We also do not try to "fix" the other person by helping them feel better or get past a negative emotion. We can encourage each other, for sure, but a negative feeling is not something to be fixed, it simply is. They won't kill us, and we will get over them. Talking about it helps us be aware that we are getting over them.

In the first year of puberty, whenever that comes, a boy will likely find it difficult to see any connection between his needs or feelings and his temptation to lust. The main reason for this is, *everything* arouses a boy during his first year of puberty. The enormous 500% increase in testosterone is simply too much to handle very well. Everywhere the boy turns, something makes him think of sex. This is even more true today where our society throws sexual images at us absolutely everywhere.

During this first year, father-son accountability may focus more on avoiding situations where the boy is confronted with things that tempt him. We still need to talk about needs and keep trying to find the connection between how we feel and when we get tempted, we just need to realize we may not make much progress.

A very helpful thing for my son was for him to text me when he felt tempted. Texting works because he is able to communicate even if I was unable to respond immediately. Just to be able to share temptation when it happened, or soon after, seemed to help a lot. Fathers should not be alarmed to find that their son they thought they had prepared so well is suddenly overwhelmed with temptation. It is not his fault, and if we keep working with them, they will improve. Eventually.

Ages 14 - 18

A year or two after puberty it seems that most boys can begin to see a correlation between their feelings and temptation to lust. This is when accountability kicks in at a new level. Father and son finally speak the same language. They can understand each other and empathize with the struggle between emotions and temptation. What was once awkward begins to feel normal. Father-son accountability becomes father-son bonding.

Continue meeting weekly. Talk about feelings more often than weekly. Make it a normal part of daily conversation. Share temptations and victories during the week as well. We don't need to save everything up for the weekly meeting. If we do, we will likely forget half of what happened.

Accountability should continue until the son is 18 for sure. Some fathers have turned accountability over to the son's responsibility at 18, entrusting him to find a peer to continue the process. Others find it better to continue, at least to some degree, even if the son finds his own accountability partner.

Father-son accountability is pretty new, so we don't know what doing this kind of thing will look like with our sons as they become adults, marry and have families. We will likely mess up a lot in the meantime, but our sons will learn even from that. Hopefully their generation will do even better than ours parenting for purity, but we still need to lay a foundation.

The Accountability Meeting

When, Where & How

When: Lucas and I meet once a week. The meeting is scheduled for Thursday night. It is not a secret meeting. If, for some reason, something comes up on Thursday night, we have our meeting Saturday or Sunday. We do not skip our accountability meeting.

Where: We go to a room in the house where we will not be overheard. It's not that we are trying to be secretive, but it is easier to be open and honest when you don't feel like the rest of the family is listening in.

How long: We may only talk for a half an hour. At first, that is about as long as we met. As we got used to meeting, we often talked for longer. As we have become more comfortable, we find we both have more we want to talk about with each other.

What to Say

Here is an outline of what my son and I do during accountability:

1. We both bring our accountability line to the meeting. We do not try remember what is on our lines from memory.
2. I start by asking how things are going. What stressful things have each of us experienced during the week? Were their times either one of us felt "unheard" or rebuked in some way.
3. Then one of us shares what is on his accountability line and which items they did and did not do. Sometimes I go first and sometimes Lucas does.
4. During sharing, we tell about times we may have been tempted to lust but we did not. These we call victories. We have found it important to recall times when we "did it right" during the week. Then we ask each other what we did that helped us not give in. This teaches us what works and helps us find successful strategies.
5. We talk more about the things we did on our "Move Toward" list than on our "Move Away From" list. We

discuss at length about how doing these things makes us feel and how motivated we are to do them.

6. We spend extra time on the "Move Away From" list if one of us has repeatedly failed for 2-3 weeks. In this case we ask each other what need is not being met and what we could do to better meet that need.

7. We each talk about the next week to see if there is anything coming that will provide added temptation. This could be something like a trip to the beach, where we will see scantily clad people running all over the place. Or it could be an unpleasant situation that one of us is facing in the near future.

How much we share: We share enough so that the other is clear what we are talking about, but nothing more. We share categories, not details. Confessing failure does not need to include the gory details.

For example, it is too general to say "I had trouble Tuesday." That does not tell enough. It is clearer to say, "I was tempted to fantasize last Tuesday," or even, "I did fantasize last Tuesday." That is enough. We do not need to find out any details about the fantasy. If someone looked at pornography, they should admit that and admit how long they were viewing it. They do not need to describe what they saw. That may cause the other person to start fantasizing themselves.

We do ask each other questions when more information is needed. If one of us says, "I had trouble," or "I struggled," the other would ask for more information. Such as, "What did you have trouble with?" As long as we do not ask for unnecessary details, questions are a good thing.

I mentioned earlier that masturbation is a topic of accountability. Let me explain further. If a father or son masturbates to fantasy or pornography, that *does* need to be disclosed. If my son says he had trouble with fantasy, it is okay to ask him if he masturbated as well. Likewise, a father should disclose to his son if he masturbates to fantasy or porn.

However, when my son began to use fantasy-free masturbation as a way to avoid lust, I tried to allow him privacy in that. He told me how often he planned to masturbate, once a week at first, but that is all I needed to know. I don't want to know when it happened or where. I didn't ask about it every week either. Once every 3-4 weeks I would ask if his masturbation was happening without fantasy. I was checking in but not asking for any details. As the frequency of his fantasy-free masturbated decreased, I stopped asking altogether. He has remained free of masturbation for a long time now, but he knows he can bring it up if it becomes a problem again.

I share nothing about sex between my wife and I with my son. That just feels a little too weird to me and Lucas has been very clear he wants to know nothing about that part of my life. I have men I am accountable with, and they are the ones to discuss that kind of thing with if I need to.

I can, however, share times when I feel unusually preoccupied with sex. Lucas is going to experience those times as well and I want him to know it is a normal thing that all men experience from time to time. I want him to see how I manage those times, which can only happen if I admit them to him.

Sharing emotions: We talk a lot about events that happened during the week and how they made us feel. Not that we get all mushy every week. We laugh a lot too. But discussing how we feel has been critical. When we let our defenses down in front of our father or son, some pretty cool things start to happen.

Lucas talks about relationships at school. I talk about relationships at work or with friends. We talk about people who disappoint us. We share feelings of being hurt or left out. We share remorse over treating others badly. We laugh at things we do and mistakes we make. We tell jokes.

The main goal of father-son accountability is to get to know each other at a level that is simply not possible any other way. A son feels truly validated as a man when his own father knows everything about him and accepts him. A father feels truly respected by his son when he can bare his soul and see that his son still loves him. This is huge. This is everything.

Who Else Knows

I realize that it is a bit unfair to ask a father to be this vulnerable with his son if he has never shared his struggle with another man. I had been attending an accountability group for a few years before my son was even born. By the time he was eleven, I was no longer afraid of sharing an account of my thought life with another man. If a father has his own struggles, he may need to join some kind of support group or form an accountability relationship with another man. A son cannot be a father's only accountability in the area of sexual purity.

My wife knows what Lucas and I talk about. In the beginning, Lucas confessed his failures to both my wife and I, not just to me. Very soon, however, he wanted to talk mainly just with me. I do not report to my wife what Lucas tells me. She knows we are dealing with the issues we need to. If something particularly alarming came up, I would make sure she did know.

My wife knows about my past struggles and failures. I divulged my secrets to her years ago. We worked through feelings of betrayal with counselors and support groups. It did take a few years for me to redirect my desires and for my wife to trust that I would remain accountable to other men.

My wife knows I am a human being, with sexual desires, and sometimes temptation happens. We are pretty honest with each other. Fortunately, these issues were resolved before Lucas and I started doing accountability. I understand not everyone will have that luxury.

Everyone has some kind of sexual baggage. Most men still have struggles at some level. It would be difficult for a father to do accountability with his son if he still held secrets about his past or present struggles his wife did not know about. It puts the son in the unfair position of choosing who to betray—divulging his father's secrets or lying to his mother.

Men who have hidden their own struggles from their wife will likely need to get help working through disclosure. I would not recommend trying this alone. A counselor would be recommended. Support and guidance from men who have worked through this would also be wise. This is not a book about marriage, but I do want to be honest and admit that father-son accountability will be severely hampered if the father is still hiding things from his spouse.

My daughter knows that my son and I do accountability. She is 19 at the writing of this book. I want her to know about what Lucas and I do. Lucas does not fear his sister knowing we do accountability. Assuming my daughter marries, she needs to know the temptations common to men. I want her to see first hand how young men are supposed to confront sexual temptation—through relationship with other men. This way, she can recognize a healthy young man when she sees one and avoid those who have not dealt with their issues.

My close friends know I do accountability with Lucas. Lucas' close friends know he does accountability with me. He has talked about it in front of everyone in his youth group. We don't put a sign in our yard saying, "Accountability in Process, Please Come Back Another Time," but we don't hide what we do either. Accountability is not something to be ashamed of, but something to be proud of.

6

CONCLUSIONS

There is much more that could be said, but who wants to read an enormous book on something so uncomfortable? Besides, this is so new that we don't really know all the answers yet. We are the pioneer generation to do this, which is pretty exciting to be a part of. The important part is that we *do* begin the journey with our sons, not that we know all the answers before we begin. It will be more valuable to discover the answers together anyway. You'll learn what works best for you, and can make modifications as you go.

Above all, be patient and don't give up. If you forget to meet once or twice, just get started again. If you feel like you are getting nowhere, keep talking. The relationship is what is important.

Make sure you spend plenty of time together when you're not talking about purity. We don't want our sons to think that's all we want to talk with them about. Spend time together doing fun things, as often as you can. That helps strengthen what you do in accountability.

I hope my son and I are still talking about purity after he's married. Hopefully he'll have his own peers to be accountable with by then, but I hope we continue at some level. I'm glad I invited Lucas into this journey with me. It has been quite an adventure so far.

ABOUT THE AUTHOR

John Fort began his career as an educator, teaching science at the secondary level for several years. Afterward, John moved into corporate training and became the Director of Technology Based Training for the eighth largest software company in the world, at the time.

Recovery from his own addiction to pornography lead John to enter purity ministry in 2008. Since then he has coordinated support group leader training for *Pure Life Alliance*, served as Northwest Regional Director for *Be Broken Ministries* and began the online ministry of *PureCommunity.org*.

He is the author of the fictional trilogy: *The Shadow of Black Rock, The Other Side of Black Rock,* and *Under the Burning Sun.* This story is an analogy of a boy falling into bondage to lust and what it took for him to become free again.

John is married with two children, Lucas being one of them, and lives in Oregon.

Lucas Fort, upon the printing of this book, is a Junior in High School. Lucas is a basketball enthusiast and throws discuss and shot put in track & field. Lucas is a serious musician and plays drums at his local church as well as in a Christian rock band.

Made in the USA
Lexington, KY
01 October 2017